FamilyFun's

GAMES ON THE GO

EDITED BY
Lisa Stiepock
and the experts at *FamilyFun Magazine*

ILLUSTRATED BY
Mark Matcho

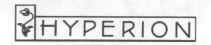

HYPERION

NEW YORK

FamilyFun's
GAMES ON THE GO

FamilyFun
BOOK EDITORS
Alexandra Kennedy and
Lisa Stiepock
MANAGING EDITOR
Priscilla Totten
ART DIRECTOR
David Kendrick
CONSULTING EDITOR
Barbara Rowley
COPY EDITORS
Paula Noonan and
Mike Trotman
EDITORIAL ASSISTANTS
Grace Ganssle, Debra Liebson,
Susan Roberts, Deborah Way
CONTRIBUTING EDITORS
Jonathan Adolph, Rani Arbo, Douglas
Bantz, Deborah Geigis Berry, Deanna
F. Cook, Ann Hallock, Amy Hamel,
Gregory Lauzon, Cindy A. Littlefield,
Vivi Mannuzza, Catherine McGrady,
David Sokol, Dana Stiepock
PRODUCTION DIRECTOR
Jennifer Mayer
TECHNOLOGY COORDINATOR
Luke Jaeger

Impress, Inc.
CREATIVE DIRECTOR
Hans Teensma
DESIGNER
Carolyn Eckert

Many of the ideas in this
book were adapted from arti-
cles in *FamilyFun* magazine.
FamilyFun is a division of
The Walt Disney Publishing
Group. To order a subscrip-
tion, call 800-289-4849.

The staffs of *FamilyFun* and
Impress Inc. conceived and
produced *FamilyFun's Games
on the Go* at 244 Main Street,
Northampton, MA 01060, in
collaboration with Hyperion,
114 Fifth Avenue, New York,
NY 10011.

Printed by Worzalla Publishing Co., Stevens Point, WI.

ISBN 0-7868-8340-5
First edition
10 9 8 7 6 5 4 3 2

This book is dedicated to FamilyFun's adventurous readers everywhere.

Special thanks to the following FamilyFun magazine writers for their wonderful ideas: Barbara Albright, Ann Banks, Lynne Bertrand, Julie Boatman, Jane Buchanan, Susan Fox, Joni Hilton, Maggie Megaw, Rebecca Lazear Okrent, Mary Jo Rulnick, Laura Purdie Salas, Jane Sanborn, Carolyn Shapiro, Candyce H. Stapen, Janet Street, Karen Telleen-Lawton, Emily B. Todd, Susan Todd, Penny Warner, and Harriet Webster.

We also extend our gratitude to FamilyFun's many creative readers who shared with us their ideas for having fun across the miles. We have credited them by name throughout the book.

We are indebted to our partners at Hyperion, especially Bob Miller, Wendy Lefkon, Kris Kliemann, David Lott, Lisa Kitei, and Robin Friedman. This book would also not have been possible without the talented FamilyFun magazine staff, who edited and art-directed many of these games and tips for the magazine from 1991 to 1998.

About our major contributors:

Carolyn Eckert is design director of Impress, Inc., the studio that produces Disney Magazine. She has designed for FamilyFun, FamilyPC, and currently designs the travel magazine Getaways.

Mark Matcho's industrial-strength illustrations can be seen in the pages of GQ, The New York Times, Entertainment Weekly, and FamilyFun. He resides in Oakland, California.

Barbara Rowley lives in Big Sky, Montana, with her husband and 2½-year-old daughter, Anna. She is a contributing editor to FamilyFun and a former camp director and teacher.

Lisa Stiepock is editor of Disney Magazine and a former travel editor for FamilyFun magazine. She cut her teeth on travel many years ago as an army brat and has been on the move ever since.

Table of Contents

On the Road Again

It's no wonder that travel has become a personal and professional passion for me. When I was growing up, my family seized every opportunity to hit the road. Whether it was a three-day weekend or a summer vacation, my parents packed up our tiny trailer, folded the four of us kids and our two dogs into the car, and headed for parts unknown. Once, my dad's job took us from New York to Kansas and we drove — taking a detour through Canada.

It didn't matter if our destination was Ann Arbor, Michigan, to visit my grandmother or Acadia National Park in Maine for some seaside camping, my dad always said his favorite part of the trip was being able to finish a conversation with his kids. Finally, we were uninterrupted by life's little necessities — going to basketball practice, washing up for dinner, taking calls from friends we just *had* to talk to. We were all liberated from our standard roles as chief cook, bottle washer, or naysayer.

Mom had a different take. She saw family travel as another chance the world was giving her to learn and to teach. We always made fun of the ratty canvas bag she carried, weighed down with the usual tissues, sunscreen, and juice drinks — as well as sixty-five pounds of library books about our destination du jour. In the car, train, or plane, or whenever we took a breather from our breakneck touring, one of us would read aloud from Mom's books. And at the end of each day, we were quizzed good-naturedly on what we'd discovered in the past twenty-four hours. (After a trip to Washington, D.C., "Roosevelt" became our standard answer to anything we didn't know.)

Looking at family travel as a chance to learn about ourselves and the places around us is what makes this book so special, and it pretty much sums up the *FamilyFun* magazine approach. Our readers, writers, and editors alike share the belief that getting there can be as much of an adventure as being there. En route, you are in a kind of cocoon, which you can look at as something to endure or something to enjoy. Kids take cues from their parents, so if you're in a playful frame of mind, they're likely to be, too.

There's another thing

that sets this book apart: family testers. Every one of the games, activities, tips, and ideas on these pages has been played, tested, and tried by real families — families like yours and mine. If it doesn't pass the *FamilyFun* real-

family test, it doesn't turn up in our pages. It must be fun, practical, and simple to set up. (If in rare cases an idea is not simple to set up, then we're telling you it is worth the time and effort.) We wanted a travel book parents could read quickly, one that would turn moods around in a pinch.

So put this in your glove

compartment, and the next time your family heads out on an expedition, dive in. You can flip to any page and start playing: there's an activity on every one, as well as scores of packing, snacking, and learning tips. Try letting your children pick their favorite ideas, or if you are looking for something in particular — a game for

kids (or parents) who get carsick, an activity to teach kids about math, or a game to play on the way to a family reunion — then head first for our indexes in the back. In any case, we hope you have as much fun using this book as we had traveling coast to coast to test it out.

Happy Trails,
Lisa Stiepock

Postcards to Me

You want your child to write; she wants mail when she gets home; and a travel journal of your trip would be something you'd both enjoy. Make it all happen by having your child record what she's done on a different postcard each day and then mail it to herself. At home, she can turn her stack of mail into a record book by punching holes in the edges of the cards and stringing them together.

MATERIALS
Postcards
Stamps
Pen

FAMILY TESTERS
Mood Music
We get our daughter to listen to classical music by putting her in charge of choosing the tapes. She then hides the cover and asks everyone else to guess the composer.

**Bonnie Coriale Figgatt
Ridgefield, Connecticut**

Clap, Tickle, Tug

It's the sitting — and sitting and sitting — that gets to kids on the road. Get their belted-in bodies moving with this game of competitive copycat. The first player makes an expression or a movement, such as a hand clap; the next player repeats that movement and adds another; and so on. Kids will be pulling on their ears, sticking out their tongues, tipping back their heads, holding their elbows — and smiling!

When a player forgets a movement, he's out. When everyone's out, start over.

NO MATERIALS NEEDED

REVVING UP
The Envelope, Please

Many of the games in this book (see pages 32, 38, and 82) require that players write numbers, letters, or words on slips of paper. You can make the transition from game to game go smoothly by preparing slips of paper ahead of time, stashing them in marked envelopes, and simply passing your kids the appropriate envelope for the game you are about to introduce.

PIT STOPS
JUMP!

At rest stops, my girls, Alethea, 9, and Nissa, 7, get out their wiggles by skipping rope while I recite rhymes from a book of jump rope jingles.

**Marie E. Plocharz
Coon Rapids, Minnesota**

Friendship Bracelets

FamilyFun editor Cindy Little-field from Massachusetts lets her daughter, Jade, while away car hours making bracelets for the pals she'll see when they reach their old hometown in Rhode Island.

To make each bracelet, gather six 24-inch strands of embroidery thread with the ends matched up, then tie an overhand knot 1 inch from an end. Tape the knot to the back of the seat in front of you. Holding the free end, twist the bunch until tightly wound. Then, pinch the twisted band in the center and fold it in half so the free end matches up with the knotted end. Release the center, and the band will twist back on itself. Tie the matched-up ends together with an overhand knot and slip the knot through the loop (the pinch point) at the opposite end of the band.

SHARING GAME

I Have Never...

Here's a quick and easy game that just might reveal some dark and not-so-dark family secrets. The first player says something he has never done, challenging everyone else to say the same, such as "I have never ridden on an airplane"; "I have never touched a frog"; "I have never eaten spinach." The object is to be the only person in the car who can say about something "I have never …"

NO MATERIALS NEEDED

I'm So Hungry I Could Eat an Alphabet

Let your half-starved brood describe just how hungry they are in this alphabet game, best played about half an hour before you plan to make a pit stop for food. This version of the I'm Packing for a Picnic game begins when you announce "I'm so hungry I could eat an aviator" ("alligator," "Alabaman," or "apple"). The next player adds on with a *B* word. She might say, for instance, "I'm so hungry I could eat an aviator and a bunny rabbit" ("belly button," "brother," or "bologna slice"). See if you can keep it up until your family is eating zoos, zippers, or zigzags.

NO MATERIALS NEEDED

REVVING UP

Essentials

The Magellan's catalog (800-962-4943) has inflatable pillows (saving graces on long trips) and a variety of light, durable travel essentials, such as hair dryers, luggage straps, alarms, adapter plugs, and clothing organizers.

The Family Portrait

Sometimes artistic inspiration is as close as the person sitting in the next seat. Turn the entire family into portrait artists and set them to work sketching each family member on a separate piece of paper. When everyone is done, mix up the sketches and then try to identify who is who. (Naturally, if your preteen has taken to describing her siblings in particularly unflattering terms, you will want to move on to another activity until her mood lifts.)

MATERIALS
Drawing paper
Pencils

At-the-Ready Activity Kit

In your battle against boredom on the road, you'll want to be armed with tools that are multi-use, flexible, creative — and don't take up too much room in the backseat. A good rule is to bring only things that can be used at least three different ways. All of these items should fit inside one lunch box. Keep the kit (you'll want one per child) in the car, replenish it after each trip, and don't play with it unless you are traveling — that way, the contents inside will stay fresh and special:

- Washable markers
- Pencils
- Pieces of cardboard for drawing surfaces
- Pencil sharpener
- Eraser
- Pad of drawing paper
- Small spiral notebook
- Stickers
- Glue stick
- Child-safe scissors
- Beads and string
- Play dough
- Egg timer
- Magnets to play with on the lid of a metal lunch box

SEARCHING GAME
Snoopy Sam

In this game of I Spy, each person gets a different list of scenarios to spot in other cars. Try to be the first to get through your list. Anyone who spots a person picking his nose automatically wins! Here are some sample situations:

- A person sitting backward
- Someone chewing gum or eating
- 6 people in one car
- 3 people in the front seat
- A woman wearing a baseball cap
- A dog on a lap
- A sleeping person

MATERIALS
Paper and pencils

AIRBORNE
Carry-ons

When we fly, we like to bring along our children's car seats for extra safety and comfort on the plane. However, lugging two heavy seats (along with luggage and two children under age 3) through a crowded airport is a nightmare. To tackle the daunting journey from parking lot to airplane, I bought two small, collapsible, luggage carts. I strap each car seat securely onto a luggage cart and then strap the children into the seats.

My husband and I can roll the kids behind us and keep one hand free for carry-on luggage. We are completely mobile, and the kids are comfortable, safely under control, and able to enjoy the fascinating backward trip through the airport and onto the plane.

Diane A. Baker
Berkeley, California

License Plate Play

There's no end to the games you can play by looking at license plates, and every family has its favorites.

LICENSE PLATE LINGO

FamilyFun *reader Barbara Moore of Las Vegas, Nevada, says her kids (Taryn, 14, Katie, 12, and Daniel, 10) like to play this game that makes wordplay out of the plates they see. The goal is to make the letters in the plate ahead make some kind of sense.*

So, if you pull up behind a car with the plate LMT 823, the first person to call out a somewhat logical phrase, such as "Love Me Tender," "Let Me Try," or "Let's Masticate Today," earns a point.

NO MATERIALS NEEDED

LICENSE PLATE 21

Don't tell your kids, but this game is really nothing more than a math addition drill. The object of 21, which is based on the card game of the same name, is to find a license plate with individual numbers that add up to or are very close to 21, without surpassing it. The plate GS 13-74 would add up to 15, for example.

One by one, players take turns counting up the

numbers on the license plate of the car that has just passed. If the license plate numbers add up to more than 21, a player will go bust on his first turn. If not, he can hold, or he can add on to his score the sum of numbers on the license plate of the next car that passes.

The player who gets closest to 21, or the player who gets 21 exactly, wins. Sighting a license plate that has the numbers 2 and 1, in that order, is an automatic victory.

WHAT'S IN A PLATE?
This game is great practice for family games of Boggle or Scrabble back home. An on-the-road word game, it requires that kids write down the letters on the first ten license plates they see, using a separate line for each tag's letters. Next, give each player five minutes to create as many words as possible from each set of letters. Letters can be added, and words can use letters in any order.

For example, with the letters *DNL*, you could get *land, drilling, dandelion,* or *Denali.* Give players ten points for every usable word; play to 100 points.

AS EASY AS A, B, C
For kids newly proud of their ability to count to 100 or say their ABC's, this game offers

an opportunity to showcase fledgling skills. All kids do is find the letters of the alphabet (in order) on car license tags. Once they've mastered this, see if they can do the same thing, only backward (from *Z* to *A*).

FAMILY TESTERS
The Kid Table
When we stop for food en route, we let our children sit at their own table and give them money ahead of time. We let them do it all themselves — from ordering to figuring out the tip.

**Joan Russell
Amesbury, Massachusetts**

KEEPSAKES
Magnetic!

Our family enjoys collecting souvenir magnets from the states we visit and using them to create a map on the side of our refrigerator. We hope one day to complete our collection after visiting all fifty states.

**Lynne Remick
Mesconset, New York**

Tall Tales

Travel Tote

Strap a shoe bag to the back of the front seat and stuff it with your small kid-entertainment supplies: crayons and coloring books; kids' magazines; craft supplies, such as pipe cleaners, markers, glue sticks, and construction paper; songbooks; paper doll kits; a deck of cards; and a cassette player with story tapes. And don't forget a Frisbee, jump rope, and chalk (to draw hopscotch grids) for rest stops.

Kids are natural spinners of tall tales, and you can put that ability to good use creating string-along stories. Bring a tape recorder with a microphone and take turns recording a tandem narrative. One person begins telling a story, but leaves it unfinished. For example, "And when the shoe did not fit, the fairy princess …" or "After the frog turned into a robo-cop, he knocked on Jessica's door only to find standing there …"

Decide in advance when the story will end (after everyone has had four turns, for instance) and then play the entire thing back.

MATERIALS
Tape recorder

GEOGRAPHY GAME

City City, Country Country

Keep up your family's moving geography lessons with this word game, which requires a fairly wide knowledge of cities and countries around the world. The object is to think of a city name that starts with the last letter of the city name stated by the previous player. The catch — after you've listed two cities, the next player can (but doesn't have to) switch to countries. After two countries,

the player can switch back to cities. In other words, you might play as follows:

CITY: Toronto
CITY: Orlando
CITY: Ottawa
SWITCH TO COUNTRY:
Albania
COUNTRY: Australia
SWITCH TO CITY:
Amsterdam
CITY: Melbourne
CITY: Enfield
Play as individuals or teams, and if you really

want to get competitive, set a time limit, such as fifteen seconds, for players to come up with answers. If a player can't, he's out, and when everyone's out, start over.

If your kids aren't old enough to have a firm grasp of the city versus country concept, then play with any place name at all.

NO MATERIALS NEEDED

PIT STOPS
My Sweet

You don't need to lug toys from the car when you stop to eat. Just grab the sugar packets on the table and try these sweet games:

Arrange twelve, sixteen, twenty, or twenty-four packets on the table in straight lines of four. Now have two players take turns removing one, two, or three packets at a time. The player who picks up the last packet loses. Or, hide an even number of pennies, nickels, dimes, and quarters under the packets and take turns trying to find matching pairs.

PACKING
HEAVIER ARTILLERY for the LONG HAUL

When your trip is more of an epic than a jaunt, you'll probably want to bring the heavy artillery. Consider packing the following in addition to your At-the-Ready Activity Kit (page 12):

- Dictionary and *The World Almanac* (resources for guessing and word games)
- Envelopes filled with scraps of paper for games (see page 9)

- Travel desk (see page 20)
- Tape recorder (see pages 22 and 33)
- Copied maps of the U.S. (see page 28)
- Felt-board travel games (see page 50)

The Great Family Mix-up

ROD TOXVONC

DOCTOR VON X

What's in a name? Anagrams, for one. Write the name of one family member at the top of a piece of paper. Then create family alter egos by rearranging the letters into silly aliases. The letters in the name Lisa Stiepock might become Sisi L. Catpoke, for instance, while Anna Perry morphs into Ape N. Yarn.

Once you've come up with your new names for everyone, have fun using them during the rest of the trip — you might require that aliases be used everytime you are in public, or whenever you are in the car. You can also develop characters for each name — Sisi L. Catpoke might be a timid cat handler, while Ape N. Yarn is a story-spinning monkey — and even use them in made up songs and stories.

MATERIALS
Paper and pencils

Mobile Show-and-Tell

Your kids always have things they want to show you, and you probably have a few treasures set aside that you'd like to share with them. Place a box or a large envelope in a central location in your home and, for the week before a trip, place items in it that you'll want the rest of your family to see. You might contribute baby photos, Dad's school papers from the third grade, a newspaper clipping about a new invention, or a really cool rock from the schoolyard. When conversation in the car turns to why sisters are stupid or to the plot of the latest teen sitcom, you can pull out your box or envelope and take turns sharing the items inside.

MATERIALS
Large envelope or box
Show-and-tell items

ROAD FOOD

TEX-MEX POPCORN

A bag of plain and simple popcorn hits the spot and makes a trip feel like an event. Make it better by experimenting with flavors. Spice it up with a sprinkle of grated cheese, pizza seasonings, onion soup mix, garlic powder, even cinnamon. Or go south of the border with this recipe:

¼	cup margarine, melted
1	tablespoon dry taco seasoning mix
½	cup popcorn kernels
2	tablespoons vegetable oil

Mix the melted margarine with taco seasoning and set aside. Pop the popcorn kernels in the oil in a large, covered pot, then pour the popped corn into a large serving bowl. Stir in the seasoned margarine and toss lightly. Makes about 8 cups.

Homemade Travel Desks

Laps are great for lots of things, but writing and drawing are not among them. Keep art projects from collapsing into your child's legs by making a custom-fitted travel desk out of a sturdy cardboard box. First, while she is seated, measure the height and width of her lap. Now, cut a half-moon big enough to comfortably fit over her legs on two opposite sides of the box and remove the bottom flaps.

If you have time, you can paint the box to dress it up and staple or glue smaller accessory boxes or envelopes to the sides for storage. You can also flip it over to store paper and other travel games inside when it's not in use.

GUESSING GAME

Am I Grammy?

On a trip to visit relatives, it's fun for your kids to find out something more than just the names and relationships of the people they'll be visiting. So tell some personal

stories in the form of a guessing game. FamilyFun *editor Jon Adolph says when his family runs out of relatives, they start guessing pets (the game is over when they get to sea monkeys).* Pick a relative and, mimicking that person's voice, tell a brief anecdote about the as-yet-nameless family member. Let everyone ask Yes or No questions until they guess who you are. Your sister may not appreciate her nephews knowing about the time she got in trouble for throwing spaghetti at you, but your kids will think it's hilarious.

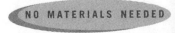

NO MATERIALS NEEDED

Keep On Trucking

Before you had kids, big trucks on the highway were just an annoyance. Now they are an event. Spark conversations with your truck-loving kids about interstate commerce, what grows where, and more. As soon as the back of a big rig, or even a small one, comes into view (and before you pull up alongside it), have everyone in the car guess what the truck has on board. Correct guesses earn the guesser a point; five points wins the game. (If you can't tell what's inside, it's a draw — no points for anyone.)

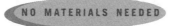

NO MATERIALS NEEDED

JAR OF LIGHT AND COLOR

On a trip to the beach, collect pebbles of different sizes, shapes, and, most important, colors. Then, collect as much beach glass as you can find, again trying to come up with as many colors as possible. Carefully wash each pebble and piece of glass and gently place them, one by one, into a clean jar. Fill the jar with water and (parents) add a spoonful of household bleach. Find a windowsill where light streams in during the day and place your jar there. It will reflect colors and light beautifully.

Make Me Laugh!

Layover Plans

If you get stuck with a long layover, give your children a portable tape recorder so they can interview family members or fellow travelers about their destinations. Also, make sure favorite travel games, toys, and books are packed in their carry-on luggage.

Nothing makes kids laugh harder than being told not to laugh. That is the premise of these make-me-giggle games, which also give your kids an excuse to be goofy on cue.

THE CAR COMIC

Designate a car comic who tells jokes, performs stupid body tricks ("Watch me touch my nose with my tongue!"), and otherwise snorts and contorts himself for a tough audience that is trying desperately not to laugh. The first person to give in to a snicker becomes the new car comic.

SALLY STRAIGHT FACE

In this variation on the same game, one person is designated Sally (or Sammy) Straight Face. All the other players take turns staring at Sally and making funny faces. As each player takes his turn, Sally must look at him and say "Sally's no Silly Willy" four times without laughing. If she laughs, the player who made her break becomes the Sally for the next round.

NO MATERIALS NEEDED

Poetry in Motion

Kids love to memorize favorite stories and poems, and a car trip offers the perfect, undistracted time in which to concentrate on the process. Rhyming stories from Dr. Seuss, Shel Silverstein, and Robert Service (*The Cremation of Sam McGee*) are particularly good memorizing material for younger kids, while the classic works of Lewis Carroll, e. e. cummings, or A. A. Milne may have more appeal for older children. As everyone commits the words to memory, they can also make up and choreograph appropriate hand motions and actions. When you are done, you've got the makings of a multimedia presentation.

MATERIALS
Favorite poetry books

TEACHING YOUR KIDS HOW TO PACK

Encourage your kids to think of mix-and-match outfits for various activities, just as they do when dressing paper dolls. (You even can have them practice by packing a doll wardrobe — trying out the different outfits — while they pack for themselves.) For example, ask a preschooler, "We're going hiking. Which of your comfortable pants do you want to wear?" After he lays these out, ask him to match them with two T-shirts (for two outfits), a sweatshirt in case it is cold, and appropriate shoes. Then, consider another vacation activity. Ask him to find two bathing suits, with a sun cover-up and a hat. Next, ask him to think about nighttime, laying out toothbrush and toothpaste, pajamas, a beloved but small stuffed animal, bathrobe, and slippers.

The Scribblers

FamilyFun *reader Abbie Nelson played these drawing games with her 5- and 6-year-old kids on a five-hour flight home to Seattle. She loved watching them play together almost as much as she loved watching their imaginations at work.*

With two people: The first person closes his eyes and scribbles on a piece of paper, then passes it to the other person who must turn it into a drawing of something real.

With more than two: The first person draws a stick figure and passes it to the next person, who adds one element — shoes, a monocle, or a belly button, for instance. The next person adds one more element and so on until your figure is deemed complete — or you run out of room on the page.

MATERIALS
Paper and pencils

REVVING UP
PET SAVVY

It's easier than ever to bring your pet along on vacation. A number of hotels now accept pets, and some even offer exercise areas and pet room service. A few go so far as to bring dog biscuits and bottled water to your room on a silver tray!

Ready Buddy for travel by making sure his ID tags are complete and by taking him on short trips close to home (so he doesn't think getting in the car means going to the vet). Try calling these hotel and motel chains to find out their pet policies: Best Western (800-528-1234); Four Seasons (800-332-3442); Holiday Inn (800-465-4329); Loews (800-235-6397); and Motel 6 (800-466-8356).

Will We See Gophers?

Another guessing game, this version centers around what you will see and do once you reach your destination. It's a great way to build excitement as you travel. To play, the leader silently picks something that the family could expect to see or do at their destination. If you are headed to Yellowstone National Park, for instance, the leader might choose anything from geysers to plastic tomahawks to horses. The other players try to determine what the leader has chosen by asking Yes or No questions that also have to do with the destination. For example, "Is it something we are going to eat?" or "Is it a place where we will sleep?"

NO MATERIALS NEEDED

AIRBORNE

Mind over Matter

When it comes to family travel to faraway places, it truly is possible to make getting there half the fun, according to *FamilyFun* contributor Candyce H. Stapen. The trick is to turn the seemingly endless airport/airplane ritual into that elusive but much valued family time. In other words, it's all in the mind-set.

Try to think of the trip itself as part of the vacation, says Stapen — get to the airport early and begin to relax. Over doughnuts in the lounge, you might hear about that special science project or how it felt to come in third at a swim team meet. On the plane, you can relate anecdotes about your own childhood (you can even bring along a small photo album or scrapbook), so your kids see you as a fellow traveler and adventurer — not only as a parent.

Travel Scrabble Plus

Travel Scrabble is a tried-and-true while-away-the-miles game. With this addition, courtesy of FamilyFun *reader Anne Lunt of Shelton, Washington, you'll make it even farther down the road.* The idea of this game is for each player to use all of the words on a completed Travel Scrabble board to come up with a story that makes sense. You'll want to give everyone at least fifteen minutes to write their Scrabble-inspired tales, then you'll need time for each person to read his story out loud.

For a shorter, easier version of the game, let players make sentences using any five words (or six or ten) on the board. Then extend the competition: add up the letters on the tiles and see whose sentence contains the most points. ("The quick brown yak jumped over the lazy xylophone"?)

For information on ordering Travel Scrabble (and replacement pieces), call Milton Bradley at 413-525-6411.

MATERIALS
Travel Scrabble game
Paper and pencils

PACKING

A HIKING CHECKLIST

If you plan any trekking, bring:
- An area map
- Canvas shoes or hiking shoes

- Long-sleeve T-shirts or sweatshirts
- Wristwatch
- Rain gear

- Hats
- Bug repellent
- Hair elastics
- Sunglasses
- Sunblock

- Flashlight
- Towelettes
- Trash bags
- Snacks
- Compass

- Water and water purification tablets
- First aid kit
- Matches

Two Truths and One Lie

FamilyFun *contributor Susan Fox offers this clever game as a way to get to* know one another even *better.* The first person tells the group three statements about herself. Two are true, and one is a lie. Everyone tries to guess which one is the lie. For example, you could say, "I won a prize in spelling in second grade. My favorite food is sushi. I got lost at the zoo when I was little." Everybody then holds up one, two, or three fingers to show which statement they think is the lie. Reveal the answer and let the next person fib away.

NO MATERIALS NEEDED

PACKING

Window Box Organizer

In the past on family road trips, I've found that keeping books and games organized and within reach (instead of under the seats) was a challenge for my boys, Joshua, 6, and Brooks, 4. I finally figured out the perfect solution: I purchased a plastic window planter and cut two parallel slits through the bottom of one end. I threaded the middle seat belt through the slits, so the box stays safely attached to the backseat. I even attached battery-operated lights (the kind you clip to books) on both sides of the box so the boys each have a lamp for reading. Best of all, the box keeps them on their own sides of the car, reducing the fight factor tremendously.

**Angela Ruder
San Antonio, Texas**

CHECK IT OUT

Read a children's book about your destination. Better yet, make your destination one that comes from a much-loved children's book. Here are a few you can check out:

If You Traveled West in a Covered Wagon by Ellen Levine (Oregon Trail)

Sacajawea and the Journey to the Pacific by Gina Ingoglia (Northwest)

Linnea in Monet's Garden by Christina Bjork (France)

Make Way for Ducklings by Robert McCloskey (Boston)

Anne of Green Gables by L. M. Montgomery (Prince Edward Island, Canada)

If Your Name Was Changed at Ellis Island by Ellen Levine (New York City)

Eloise by Kay Thompson (New York City)

Road Map Mania

AMERICA THE BEAUTIFUL
With this simple game that works for toddlers and teens, FamilyFun *reader Peggy Krueger of North Ridgeville, Ohio, incorporates a little geography lesson into her family trips.* On a copy of a U.S. map, have your kids color in each state as they spot the license plate for it.

Obviously, this activity can take a day or a lifetime, but when attentions start to wane, you can keep kids' interest by reading various facts from an almanac about the states you've already spotted. Older kids can list on their maps three points of interest for each colored-in state.

You can also try a short version of this game by giving players a list of only ten states (ones you're likely to see plates for) to color in.

> **MATERIALS**
> Copied maps of the
> United States (at least
> two per player)
> Colored markers
> *The World Almanac*
> (optional)

LOST AND FOUND
In this two-person game, turn an ordinary road map into a treasure hunt — and give your kids valuable lessons in map reading. To play, one person finds a destination — city, park, road intersection, whatever —

on the road map. She tells the other player what type of thing to look for and then hands her the map, giving her sixty seconds to find the exact spot. If player two succeeds in locating it, she gets a point. If she doesn't, player one gets the point. Players take turns finding destinations, and the first person to get to ten points wins. With young players or beginning readers, you might consider lengthening the search time or giving clues to narrow down the search area.

> **MATERIALS**
> Watch with second hand
> Road map

FOLLOW THE YELLOW BRICK ROAD

Tourism brochure racks are great sources for new games: you can almost always find free maps there of places you've yet to explore. Grab some maps from the racks at your hotel and spend a few minutes before bed turning them into treasure hunts, a perfect activity for the restaurant or car. First, find one destination and circle it, labeling it "Start." Now, find — but don't mark — the place where you want the kids to finish. Trace a circuitous route from the start to finish with your finger, marking down points along the way on a separate piece of paper. A typical treasure hunt might include the following directions.

- Start at Billings
- Go west at the first airport sign
- Cross a bridge
- Turn right at the first crossroad following the second rest stop
- Continue past the national monument
- Go ten miles south on Highway 191

When your kids believe that they have followed your directions correctly, have them circle what they think their destination was. Reveal your answer. Then have them make up treasure maps for each other. Soon they'll be adept enough at map reading to be backseat navigators.

MATERIALS
Extra road maps

Make a Machine

Turn your family into a finely tuned machine in this copycat game (with a twist). Play begins when one family member makes a machinelike movement (wrist twist, knee jerk, and so on) with an accompanying creak, hiss, or groan. The next player repeats the first player's motion and sound, then adds a different noise and motion of her own. Soon the entire family is roaring, squeaking, and chugging like a not-so-well-oiled machine. Play continues until someone misses a motion or sound or the entire enterprise falls apart into laughter.

NO MATERIALS NEEDED

AIRBORNE

The Earache Solution

You can often lessen ear discomfort on airplanes by nursing infants, giving tots bottles or pacifiers, and letting older kids chew gum (buy it on your way to the airport because many terminals do not sell chewing gum — workers are tired of cleaning it off floors and chairs). But if your child experiences real ear pain, you can try this funny-looking but often effective trick. Ask the attendant for two plastic cups. Fold a napkin into the bottom of each cup and pour in just enough hot water to moisten the napkins. Then, place the cups over your child's ears, making sure you hold them tightly against his head.

Radio Bingo

Wouldn't it be nice to actually hear *the radio as you drive along? Get your kids to quiet down and tune in with this game, which rewards the careful ear.* To play, draw one Bingo board for each player, making twenty-five squares — five across and five down — on sheets of paper. In each square, write a word that you are likely to hear on the radio: *news, weather, traffic, president, Washington, New York, Dow Jones, Hollywood, today, yesterday, bargain, sale, love, heart, wish, dog, cry,* and so on. Hint: You'll court the most humor and competition if you give each board a few words that are found on that board only. (If you like, you can make up several boards in advance and get them copied before you travel.)

Pass out the boards and ask everyone to listen attentively, interrupting their radio reverie only when they hear one of the words on their board and are able to mark it off with a pencil. Of course, they'll also want to make a noisy announcement when they actually get Bingo — lining up five in a row across, down, or diagonally.

This is a fun game that you and your kids can rework to play again and again.

> **MATERIALS**
> A working radio
> Paper and pencils

PIT STOPS
Dandelion Chains

Collect dandelions — about twenty-five of them — at a rest stop and weave a crown when you get back in the car. It's easy. With a fingernail, make a quarter-inch slit in each stem, 2 inches below the blossom. Slip the next flower's stem through the slit and pull it until you get to the flower head. Do the same with the next and the next until you've made a chain the right length for your child to wear.

31

Color-Coded

FamilyFun reader Susan Robins of Cottage Grove, Oregon, made up this road game, which is a surefire bet with her 4-year-old, Timmy. Write each letter of the alphabet on variously colored construction paper cards. Or, use scraps of plain paper and write down both a letter and a color on each. Each player picks a card and searches for an object that matches the color and begins with the letter on that card. A person who has a *B* on a yellow card might spot a field of buttercups, for example. "Timmy remembers more details of our travels," says Susan, "and instead of hearing 'Are we there yet?' when we get close, we hear 'Oh no, I haven't found mine yet!'"

MATERIALS
Construction or plain paper
Pencil

(also see page 72)

CLASSICS

WANDA THE WIZARD #1

Wanda the Wizard has some real tricks up her sleeve (also see page 72). Try them out on your kids or let an older sibling play with a younger one.

Whoever is the wizard tells her subject that she has the power to guess any date — birthday, holiday, whatever. She gives him a piece of paper and a pencil and instructs him to:

1. Think of a date numerically (July fifth would be 7/5).
2. Multiply the number of the month by 5.
3. Add 6.
4. Multiply the answer by 4.
5. Add 9.
6. Multiply the answer by 5.
7. Add the day of the month.
8. Ask him to tell you the result. Subtract 165 from it and, voilà, reveal the date (705 in this case — when the month is one digit, ignore the zeros).

The Family Tree

All you need is a tape recorder and some long-term memory for this game, a telling way to get ready for a family reunion. Give your kids a tape recorder with a handheld microphone and let them interview you about your immediate- and extended-family history. If time permits, have your kids turn the interviews into an illustrated storybook that you can photocopy and distribute to reunion-goers (select details excepted, of course!).

MATERIALS
Tape recorder
Paper and crayons
(optional)

REVVING UP
Following Along

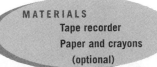

Last year, my family traveled 2,000 miles by car on three trips with our 4-year-old daughter, Julie, and 3-year-old twins, Jonathan and Megan. Of all the books, games, and toys that I brought, a homemade activity — personalized read-along storybooks recorded on cassette — proved to be the most entertaining. I made up a story to prepare my kids for a family reunion and bound the pages in three-ring binders. Then I read it onto a cassette tape, adding songs, poems, and favorite tales.

One of the tunes taught each child to sing her name and address; another, a rap song, rhymed with the digits in our phone number.

The kids particularly enjoyed responding to questions I incorporated into the stories and songs. I've made a number of tapes and stories now. On the most recent one, I accidentally recorded a conversation between my oldest daughter and me — it turned out to be the kids' favorite part.

Nancy A. Giehl, Spring, Texas

Poodle Me, Please!

Ask your kids to "Please poodle down now" and you're certain to have their attention. It probably won't take much more explanation to teach them the Poodle game, as they will probably have already guessed that you are substituting *poodle* for *quiet*. The idea is to come up with a verb and substitute for it the word *poodle*.

One player should close her eyes while everyone else writes down verbs until they've agreed on one. The guessing player then asks all the other players questions to determine what word they have chosen by substituting the word *poodle* where that verb would be: "Can I poodle on a train?" "Would I poodle by the side of the road?" "Do little sisters poodle?" "Do poodles poodle?" The guesser gets one point for every question she has to ask until she guesses the verb. At the end of a predetermined number of rounds, the player with the lowest number of points wins.

MATERIALS
Paper and pencils

Mr. Mom

Warning: This activity is decidedly addictive. Bring along a Polaroid camera and, while eating at a rest stop, take each person's picture in the exact same sitting or standing position (and from the exact same vantage point).

Once you are back in the car, use safety scissors to cut the pictures in half horizontally. You can then shuffle your family's faces and torsos (if the pictures were taken from a distance) or the top and bottom halves of their faces (if you took close-ups). If you're feeling particularly creative, you can paste each picture onto a piece of paper, cut the paper along the same horizontal lines, and secure it in a loose-leaf binder to form your own Family Mix and Match book. Any way you slice it, this activity is worth the effort.

MATERIALS
Polaroid camera
Scissors

COUNTING THE MILES

Last summer, we set out on our first big road trip. To get us through the first long day of driving (500 miles), I strung a long string with a marble-size bead for every twenty-five miles we would travel. Every fourth bead was a white bead. As we completed each twenty-five miles, the children moved a bead to the other end of the string. Our children could visualize how far we had to go by how many beads were left. After 100 miles, the white bead was moved, signaling a treat from Mom's Bag. Every day, our kids stayed occupied counting the beads, comparing how far we had come to how far we had to go. Our first grader added the twenty-fives and informed us often of our progress.

Jane Rice
Maple Grove, Minnesota

Conversation Starters

Time on the road offers families the perfect opportunity to reconnect by having conversations that don't revolve around car pools, chores, or eating all your vegetables. If you have trouble switching conversational gears, try asking your kids these questions or similar variations. You can give them the wheel sometimes, too, letting them ask you probing queries! Or you can turn this less-than-idle chat into a game by writing questions on slips of paper, placing them in a hat, and passing the hat — the question you pick out is the one you must answer, honestly.

Make your queries silly or serious, but be sure they cannot be answered by just saying Yes or No.

- If you could make up a holiday, what would it be and how would you celebrate it?
- What is the first thing you would do if you became president?
- Would you rather be a butterfly or a fish? Why?
- Do you think dogs are smarter than cats? Are dogs smarter than horses?
- What did settlers on the prairie have for breakfast 100 years ago? What will we be eating for breakfast in 100 years?
- If you had to lose one of your five senses, which would it be? Which one sense would you choose if you could only have one? Why?

- Would you like to have sonar like a bat, or be able to run as fast as a gazelle? Why?
- If you could choose five animal qualities for yourself from the animal kingdom, what would they be?
- Who is your best friend, and what qualities does she have that you like?
- Who is your favorite famous person and why?
- What's the silliest thing you ever did?
- Discuss something you did yesterday.
- Tell something embarrassing about yourself.
- What is the best book you've read recently, and why did you like it?
- What will you do this summer?
- What's your earliest memory?
- What do you think the surface of the moon looks like?
- Where should we go for spring break next year?
- If you were going to write a book, what would it be about?
- What will you be doing in ten years?
- If you discovered a new island, what do you imagine would be on it?
- Who is your hero and why?
- What one thing would you change about school?
- What should we surprise Mom with for her birthday this year?
- If Spider-Man and Batman fought, who would win and why?
- Discuss something fun you have done in the past couple of days.
- What is the best — and the worst — thing you have ever eaten?
- What is an item of international news that you have heard or read about in the past few months?
- If Barney and Big Bird played basketball, who would win and why?

NO MATERIALS NEEDED

ROAD FOOD
Sun Munchies

2	cups sunflower seeds
1	cup pumpkin seeds
1	cup raisins
1	cup pine nuts
1	cup dried cranberries

Place in a plastic bag, shake, and serve.

Animal Charades

Even preschoolers can enjoy this lively game, which lets them practice the animal sounds they know and add a few more to their repertoire. Players take turns imitating an animal, while everyone else attempts to guess what manner of beast they are hearing. The person with the correct guess becomes the animal mimic for the next round. To add more challenge, write down names of animals on slips of paper and have players draw a slip and imitate that creature.

Once the car becomes too zoolike, try the whole exercise as mimes, with players imitating animals by soundlessly mimicking their faces and motions.

NO MATERIALS NEEDED

FAMILY TESTERS
Pretzel Twist

Toss a bag of pretzels into the backseat and challenge your kids to bite out every letter of the alphabet.

**Susan Fox
Palo Alto, California**

CLASSICS
No End

In this word game, the object is to spell out a word in turns, letter by letter, without being the one to finish it. For example, the first person might say *P*, the second *O*, and the third *C* (but not *P* or *T*, which would finish words). Have a real word in mind (*pocket*), or you can be challenged.

The Model Has Two Faces

One of the things this quick and revealing exercise shows kids is that faces are rarely symmetrical. To play, find a magazine photograph of a full face looking at the camera. Cut the photo in half (straight down the center of the nose), tape it to a piece of paper, and let your child draw in the missing half of the face.

When he is finished, let him compare his drawing to the other half of the photograph.

MATERIALS
Magazines
Safety scissors
Glue stick or tape
Paper
Crayons or pencils

Top Air Travel Tips

- Book early for good seats.
- Order kids' meals when you make your reservation.
- Stuff your carry-on for every contingency: pack medications, extra kids' clothes, diapers, baby food, and formula. And be sure the kids' toys are in their carry-ons.
- Bring international currency for overseas layovers.
- Make each child who is old enough responsible for his own luggage.
- Check luggage curbside.
- Let kids work off energy in the lounge — save sleepy moments for the plane.
- To quell plane fears, explain each step of the flight to first-time fliers so they understand that sudden noises and shaking do not signal an imminent crash.
- Locate pillows and blankets as soon as you board.

News from the Road

CLASSICS
A Tougher Tic-tac-toe

Make the classic game of tic-tac-toe a little more lively and a bit tougher with this one basic change: with each turn, a player can fill in the empty space of his choice with either an *X* or an *O*.

Whether they are playing biographer or reporter, kids love the idea of recording everything they see and do. Instead of individual trip diaries this time, encourage your kids to "publish" news from the road. Give them reporter's notebooks and pencils, even a tape recorder, and let them spend the time between destinations writing down or recording details about the people they've met, seen, or interviewed.

At the end of each day, have them turn their observations into a paper — complete with breaking news ("Jeff removes tick from family dog"), movie, book, and restaurant reviews (a comparison chart of the best service and food at rest stops), sports analysis ("Did Dad cheat during yesterday's bowling match?"), profiles ("Last night's innkeeper grew up in Germany …"), weather reports, horoscopes, even editorial columns ("Ask Mom!"). They can write on drawing paper and add illustrations or Polaroid pictures. Then, just ask the hotel office to make a few photocopies and pop them in the mail to friends and relatives.

MATERIALS
Reporter's notebooks
Pencils
Tape recorder (optional)
Paper

Add-on Vacation Collage

Instead of cluttering up the car with ticket stubs, brochures, and dried flowers, collect vacation mementos as you tool along and have your kids turn them into a snappy poster. To make a vacation mural, just keep a tube of glue and a piece of poster board in the trunk. When you empty your kids' pockets and packs each night, take pieces of the day's treasures — maps, place mats, even sand, sticks, or pieces of mica — and glue them onto the poster board. Once your kids get the hang of it, they'll start looking for additions as you travel. Back at home, you can cover the mural with glass or clear Con-Tact paper for a suitable-for-framing travel souvenir.

MATERIALS
Poster board
Glue

KEEPSAKES
Vested Interests

My son, Jesse, 6, especially likes to go to places where he can learn about history and nature. Most of the museums and parks we visit sell emblem patches for a few dollars. Jesse collects these, and I sew them on his "travel vest." Now, Jesse remembers the place and not just a souvenir toy. He's known at school for his travel adventure stories.

Michelle Winecoff, Gastonia, North Carolina

Homemade Erasable Sketch Pads

My kids like to draw with wet-erase and dry-erase marker and pad sets, but these get expensive. I found an inexpensive way to let them draw to their hearts' content: I bought a packet of plastic loose-leaf paper covers and one clipboard for each child. The kids can slip a piece of paper into the cover, secure it with the clipboard, and draw away. They can put anything inside the covers, from plain white paper to blank mazes to pages from coloring books. The washable ink just wipes off the plastic, and the paper can be reused or replaced whenever the kids like.

**Sheila Phillips
Fresno, California**

Count-'em-up Scavenger Hunts

Scavenger hunts are a great way to get your kids' eyes away from their pocket computer games and back on the world outside the car windows. The rules are simple: for competitive play, just be the first to call out what you've seen and you can cross it off your list; ties mean sightings go to both players. For team play, just search and eliminate collectively.

These lists feature fairly easy-to-spot items, but because they require you to find a number of each item, they work best when everyone in your family is searching together.

COUNT-'EM-UP HUNT 1

You should be able to find these items when driving through populated areas.

 2 in-line skaters
 1 train
 1 white bird
16 wheels with spokes
 2 dead trees
 1 Bicycle Crossing sign
 3 school buses
12 sports cars
 6 animals in cars
 1 mural or billboard
 2 wooden fences
 1 abandoned shack
 1 moped or tandem bike
 5 strollers
 4 coffee shops
 3 Dead End signs
11 lawn ornaments

COUNT-'EM-UP HUNT 2

This list is perfect to use on a stretch of seemingly barren highway.

1 25-mph sign
10 minivans
2 rivers
1 town named after a president
3 abandoned cars
25 cows
1 antique car
4 horses
3 trailer homes
5 bulldozers, cranes, steamrollers, or plows
1 bumper sticker you think is funny (write it down)
1 bumper sticker you disagree with and why (write it down)
1 Falling Rocks sign
5 trucks carrying food products
1 dead muffler

COUNT-'EM-UP HUNT 3

Use this short list when you are driving at night.

1 blinking light
5 Exit signs
4 motels
3 fast-food restaurants
1 star
9 overpasses
7 gas stations
2 emergency phones
1 car with one headlight

MATERIALS
Paper and pencils

ROAD FOOD

SANDWICH ROLL-UPS

FamilyFun food editor Deanna Cook suggests letting your kids help you create these tubular twisters. They travel well and make even PB & J seem novel.

Slices of soft bread
Any of these fillings:
    Peanut butter and jelly
    Sliced turkey and cranberry sauce
    Cream cheese and jelly
    Sliced ham and Swiss cheese
    Refried beans, shredded cheese, and salsa
    Grated cheese and chopped tomatoes
    Tuna salad
    Cheese and sweet relish

Simply flatten the bread slices, then roll your favorite fillings inside. The only trick is to ensure that the bread is malleable enough to roll up without breaking. Use soft, fresh bread and sprinkle each slice with a few drops of water. Cut off the crust, place it between two pieces of waxed paper, and flatten slightly with a rolling pin. Place a thin layer of filling on each of the slices and then roll up, being careful not to tear the bread. Cover the twisters tightly with plastic wrap or foil to prevent the bread from drying out.

Where in the World?

You'll need players with a fair amount of geographic expertise (or The World Almanac) to play this version of Twenty Questions. The leader picks a country (or state, city, or other destination), and the other players take turns asking questions (up to twenty) that can be answered with a simple Yes or No in order to decipher the answer.

("Do lemurs live here?" "Yes." "Madagascar!") If you are playing with *The World Almanac,* both the leader and the other players can use it for answering and asking questions. Whoever discovers the answer first becomes the next leader.

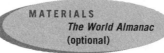

MATERIALS
The World Almanac
(optional)

ROAD FOOD
SHORE SNACKS

Make this sea food for your journey to the beach. You'll love this mix because it's healthy, light, a cinch to prepare, and it won't spoil in the heat. Children will enjoy pretending the ingredients are seaside finds.

1 cup dry chow mein noodles (seaweed)
1 cup pretzel sticks (driftwood)
1 cup fish crackers
1 cup dried pineapple (sea glass)
1 cup raisins (fish eggs)

1 cup roasted peanuts (beach pebbles)
1 cup Cheerios (life preservers)

Combine all ingredients in a large plastic bag and shake.

PIT STOPS
Energy Releasers

Six top games to beat the fidgets:
- Leapfrog
- Four Square
- SPUD
- Tag
- Frisbee
- Wheelbarrow Races

A Is for *Armadillo*

This is a terrific game to play with preschoolers. More populated areas yield more interesting results. The leader picks a letter and announces it to the other players, who then join the leader in competing to find three things (both in and out of the car) that start with the designated letter. Choose *A*, for example, and you might spot an armadillo, an automobile, and an apple. The first person to succeed gets to choose the next letter.

NO MATERIALS NEEDED

CLASSICS

And Don't Forget . . .

- Connect the Dots (draw your own)
- Name That Tune (use your car radio or sing)
- Rock, Paper, Scissors
- Thumb wrestling
- Hangman
- Making paper-clip chains
- Folding newspaper hats
- Telling knock-knock jokes

Make-Your-Own Puzzle Maps

You can teach your kids about the states you'll be traveling through without spending money on fancy toys. Create a puzzle by covering a map of the United States with a sheet of clear Con-Tact paper, making sure the surface is smooth. Then, have your child cut out the states and practice putting the map back together.

To turn your puzzle into a game, write the state names on slips of paper along with bits of information, such as "Arkansas is known for its diamonds and quartz crystals." Put the slips into a hat. Then let your child turn the states face down, pick a slip and read the trivia, and then try to identify the state that goes with it by its shape.

Guess My Name

Kids are natural mimics, as you no doubt found out early on when your toddler started displaying your mannerisms, good and bad. Put this talent to work in a less public way in this acting game, which requires that players imitate the motions, habits, and/or expressions of a famous person, such as an athlete, a politician, a musician, or an actor. The clincher: No talking allowed! Players can ask Yes or No questions (which are met by a nod or a shake). The first guesser with a correct answer does the next impression.

NO MATERIALS NEEDED

Family Trivia

Back in the eighties when Trivial Pursuit was the rage, teacher Lynn Bonsey of Surry, Maine, and her sister Lorna Healey of Litchfield, Maine, came up with It's All Relative, a homemade version based on their often hilarious family history. Playing it has become a family tradition. Here's how to make up your own game. First decide on a number of categories, such as People We've Known; Places We've Been; Events and Happenings; Relatives; and, of course, Miscellany. Pick a different color of index card for each category, then have everyone write questions on the front and answers on the back of the appropriately colored cards. Questions should be intimate to the family, such as "How many stuffed animals did Taryn throw out of a moving car?"; "Which two high school boyfriends did Aunt Heidi and Aunt Dana share?"; "How did Austin lose his front tooth?"; "In what resort town did we first taste lobster?"

Next print the letters in the phrase "It's All Relative" separately on bits of index cards many times over and place them in a container.

When a player correctly answers a question, he draws from the container of letters. The first to collect all the letters in "It's All Relative" wins.

Back home, you can use your cards to create a board game, and add photographs to ask questions about. (You can order a copy of Lynn and Lorna's book of game instructions, titled *It's All Relative: How to Create Your Own Personal Family History Trivia Game,* by calling 207-667-2968.)

MATERIALS
Colored index cards
Pens or markers

CLASSICS

SOMETHING FISHY

Show your kids a picture of this fish and ask them to draw it without lifting their pencils or retracing any lines. (Hint: Go up a fin first, then down.) Once they've mastered Finned Freddy, challenge them to make up some one-line pictures of their own.

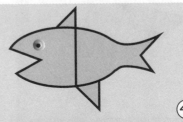

CLASSICS
Tricky Triangles

Draw triangles like the one below and ask your kids to count the triangles inside (we found seventeen in this one).

Draw That Tune

Music has inspired many great artists. See how it moves your young Picassos. Sing standards, or turn the radio on and let your kids draw whatever they hear. Oldies and country stations seem to work best: Kids won't automatically know all the words, so they'll have to listen quietly, and you won't worry about lyrics you wouldn't want to see illustrated by anyone — particularly by your own children.

Some of these old lyrics are the silliest to draw — did you ever wonder what Benny and the Jets, Lucy in the Sky, or Superfly looks like? Others can be misinterpreted in a way that's more hysterical than motivational. You might find your kids have drawn a bathroom on the right (instead of a "bad moon on the rise") or Michael rowing his boat ashore to get a noodle ("Hallelujah!").

MATERIALS
Drawing paper
Markers or crayons
A working radio

Foil Boredom

This one is so simple you won't believe it. There are no rules and no directions. Just pull over to the nearest convenience store, buy a roll of aluminum foil, and toss it into the backseat. Although foil is hardly a traditional sculpture material, it works. In the hands of your kids, aluminum foil can be turned into snakes, crowns, masks, and more. (You might need to switch activities when it turns into a bat and balls.)

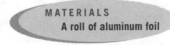

MATERIALS
A roll of aluminum foil

PACKING
Beach Checklist

- Blanket
- Chair

- Umbrella
- Pails
- Shovels
- Sifters
- Flippers
- Mask or goggles

- Snorkel tube
- Inflatable raft
- Bodyboard
- Frisbee disc or football
- Paddleball
- Sunscreen

- Sunglasses
- Towels
- Cover-ups
- Hats
- Magazine or novel
- Towelettes

- Cooler stocked with sandwiches, fruit, individually wrapped snacks, and beverages, including plenty of water

Felt Factory

With little more than felt and cardboard, you can make up a slew of kids' travel games. Here are a few that have passed the FamilyFun *reader-enjoyment test with flying (and driving) colors.*

WHAT'S SHAPING UP

Felt storyboards take only a few minutes and a few dollars to create, so make one for every child traveling. For each one, you'll need:

  1 shoe box
  Sheets of felt in
     different colors
  Scissors
  Glue

First glue a piece of felt onto the inside of a shoe box lid. Then, out of variously colored felt pieces, cut circles, rectangles, triangles, squares, and other shapes (you can use cookie cutters as guides) to store inside the shoe box. Challenge kids to create objects on their storyboard lid. Can they make a dinosaur? How few shapes do they need to fashion a recognizable pig? Who can build the most buildings?

    Once they tire of that, they can host a one-dimensional puppet show. Suggest that they retell a fairy tale, such as "Goldilocks and the Three Bears" or "Jack and the Beanstalk."

FELT GOOD GAMES

Pocket-size travel games are great, but they do have limitations, as anyone knows who has spent time sticking his fingers in seat cracks searching for a pencil-eraser-size checkers piece.

You can make your own felt board games for less than $5 and in about 15 minutes.

For a two-games-in-one set of checkers and five-in-a-row, you'll need:

- 1 8½- by 11-inch piece of box-weight cardboard
- 2 sheets of self-adhesive white felt trimmed to the same size

Scissors

- 1 black permanent marker

Ruler, pencil

- 2 squares each of red and black felt (nonadhesive)
- 1 10- by 15-inch manila mailing envelope

Checkerboard: Apply the white felt to both sides of the cardboard. Using a pencil and ruler, draw an 8- by 8-inch square, then divide the square into eight 1-inch squares across and down. Starting with the top row and the left-hand square, color in every other square black as you move across, line by line. Then, using a quarter as your pattern, cut the red and black felt into thirty-two circles in each color. If you have felt left over, make a few extra: these are the easiest game replacement pieces you'll ever find.

Five-in-a-row: Now turn the other side of your board into a five-in-a-row game board. Draw a 5- by 5-inch square and divide it into twenty-five 1-inch squares, five across and five down. For this game, no squares are colored in. The object of this advanced version of tic-tac-toe is to get five of your pieces lined up either horizontally, diagonally, or vertically — and for the other player to try to block you. Use your checkers pieces for this game as well. Store your felt circles and board in a 10- by 15-inch manila envelope.

Around the World in 30 Cars

You may be traveling domestically, but there's no reason your kids can't learn a little global geography along the way. Search cars for the oval stickers with letters that denote foreign countries (see thirty examples below). Then engage your kids in a little wishful vacation thinking. What would Dad like to do in Belgium?

Would any kids dare to eat raw fish in Japan? If you have *The World Almanac*, use it to brainstorm what the country would be like, where you'd go, and what you'd do and eat each day.

A	Austria
AUS	Australia
B	Belgium
CDN	Canada
CH	Switzerland
CR	Costa Rica
D	Germany
DK	Denmark
E	Spain
F	France
GB	Great Britain
GR	Greece
H	Hungary
HK	Hong Kong
I	Italy
IRL	Ireland
IS	Iceland
J	Japan
L	Luxembourg
M	Malta
MC	Monaco
MEX	Mexico
N	Norway
NL	Netherlands
P	Poland
S	Sweden
TR	Turkey
USA	United States
V	Vatican City
YV	Venezuela

MATERIALS
The World Almanac
(optional)

The Hairy Hamburger

Refresh your kids' basic grammar and give them fodder for their next drawing with this activity. Working as a family, write down ten adjectives on separate pieces of paper and place them in a cup. Choose those that refer to physical or behavioral characteristics that you can see, such as *green, sweaty,* or *prissy* — the more over-the-top the better. Then write ten nouns — again, weird is good — on separate pieces of paper and place them in a different cup. Let each child pick one scrap from each cup; then have them draw the combo they've created. Expect yucky alligators, grungy teachers, and, yes, — hairy hamburgers. For even more complex

drawings, pick two adjectives for every noun and get slippery flying tomatoes.

MATERIALS
Writing paper
Pencils
Drawing paper
Markers or crayons

COPILOTS

A MAP OF HIS OWN

Whenever our family sets out on a road trip, my husband and I trace out the planned route for our 11-year-old son, David, and our 8-year-old daughter, Caytlin. Using AAA maps, I cut out the portion that pertains to our trip and glue it to a piece of cardboard. (Depending on how much area our journey will cover, I sometimes use both sides of the cardboard to display the map.) My husband highlights the roadways with a marker, then we cover the map with a sheet of clear Con-Tact paper.

Besides being a big hit with the kids, the map is a ready reference for the driver. Although long stints in the car can be hard on kids (and adults), we have learned that when everyone is interested in following the route, the trip can be a special time spent together as a family.

Annette Payne
Santa Barbara, California

Under Cover

When my husband and I started traveling with our 6-year-old son and 4-year-old daughter, I made a plaid, flannel blanket for each of them. I sewed two layers of cloth together and appliquéd labels — "Alan's Travels" and "Kelly's Travels." Not only do the blankets keep the kids warm during naps in the car, but now, covered with souvenir patches from zoos, state forests, and other vacation spots, they also are sweet reminders of all the fun times we have had.

Alan and Kelly enjoy deciding where each new patch will be sewed on, and their blankets always are the first things to be put in the car when we are getting ready for a trip.

Kathy Smith Anthenat
Reminderville, Ohio

More Conversation Starters

Is there a lull in the conversation (or has it turned into a contact sport?). Try asking your kids these probing questions (see page 36 for more).

- What do humans look like to monkeys?
- What is your favorite flower?
- What is the best place you have ever been?
- Who is your most interesting relative and why?
- What's the most exciting thing that happended at your school last year?
- If you could pick one celebrity to teach your class for a day who would it be?

NO MATERIALS NEEDED

Color Safari

This all-ages game is easily adaptable to your kids' attention spans and the amount of time you have to play. All you do is agree on a basic color — such as red, blue, green, or yellow — and challenge your kids to find 100 items that are this color. Younger kids can play a shortened version — counting items to ten or even twenty-five; older kids will be challenged if you set a time limit and make them race against one another. You can also give each player a different color to search for.

NO MATERIALS NEEDED

FAMILY TESTERS
BACKSEAT PILOTS

"I'm bored" rarely is heard during our annual 2,500-mile excursion to our family's reunion. My 7-year-old son, Michael, and my 8-year-old twin daughters, Alexis and Nicole, share their grandfather's passion for flying gliders. Gramps's backseat workshop consists of a 12- by 18-inch piece of gypsum board for a work surface and a small zippered bag that holds Whitewings airplane parts and directions, child-safe scissors, clamps, glue, a glider launcher, rubber bands, and bond paper for making folded planes. The miles fly by while the kids are cutting, gluing, clamping, and customizing. Before we realize it, it's time for a pit stop and a test flight.

By the end of our trip, we often have a fleet of six to eight Whitewings gliders, a dozen folded and decorated paper planes, and six family members looking forward to our next cross-country trek.

Christine Carter, Piscataway, New Jersey

Draw-Your-Own Postcards

When she was an art teacher in Hudson, Iowa, FamilyFun *reader Debra Roach had her students create handmade postcards. Now her daughter, Kelly, carries on the tradition, drawing fish cards for Dad, horses for Grandpa, and cats for her friends.* You can buy blank mailing notes at arts and crafts stores or make your own out of cardboard. As you drive along, let your kids create their own postcards of familiar trip scenery — a distant mountain, a covered bridge, or, as is often the case, the back of Dad's head.

MATERIALS
Blank postcards
Crayons or markers

The Best Card Games for the Road

If you bring one game or toy on a vacation, it might well be a deck of cards. The games you can play and make up are endless and can be tai-lored to any age. The only problem is the bumps in the road (or, heaven forbid, the air). You can order magnetic cards (call Kling Mag-netics at 800-523-9640) or try these road-safe games. See page 58 for instructions for Old Maid. If you don't remember how to play the others, check out a card games book, such as *The Book of Cards for Kids* by Gail MacColl.

- Beggar My Neighbor
- Go Boom
- Go Fish
- Hit or Miss
- Old Maid
- Sequence
- Snap and Baby Snap
- War (or Slapjack)

CRAFT

Memory Box

*For FamilyFun reader
Deborah Bydlon of Juneau,
living in Alaska has led to
some long car trips back
to the "lower forty-eight."
On these treks, her sons,
Matthew and Christopher,
bring along souvenir travel*
kits they make out of shoe
boxes. Cover a shoe box
with stickers and drawings
and let your kids fill it with
vacation treasures along
the way. They can collect
brochures, ticket stubs,
takeout menus, postcards,
feathers, leaves, and so on.
(You may want to limit
the number of rocks they
can bring home!)

MATERIALS
Shoe box
Stickers or markers

PACKING
Mr. Lauzon's Camping List

FamilyFun staff writer Greg
Lauzon's parents kept travel costs
down by taking their five boys
camping. Tested many times over,
here is Greg's dad's packing list.

1. Tent(s)
2. Sleeping bags
3. Plastic ground cloth
4. Camp stove
5. Pots, plastic dishes,
   and utensils
6. Bottle and can openers
7. Sharp knife (in custody
   of parents)
8. Water and water purifiers
9. Stocked coolers
10. Lantern, candles, matches
11. Flashlights, extra batteries
12. Toilet paper
13. First-aid kit, sunscreen,
    insect repellent, medications
14. Day packs for hiking; child
    carriers for babies and toddlers
15. Compass and area map
16. Plenty of plastic bags

Mad, Sad, Glad

OLD MAID

Don't remember how to play one of the best card games for the road? Here are the directions for Old Maid.

First, remove the queen of spades from the deck. Then deal out the rest of the cards one by one facedown among players (it doesn't matter if some players get more than others). Each player should look at her cards and remove pairs (pairs of number, not color or suit — an 8 of spades and an 8 of hearts are a pair). Place the pairs facedown in a pile in front of you. The first player to the dealer's left asks the player to his left to hold up her cards facing inward. He then picks a card from her hand and if it makes a pair, places it on his pile. If not, he keeps it. The next player goes and so on. The loser is the player who is stuck with a lonely queen, the Old Maid.

At the end of an activity-packed vacation day, check in with everyone using this simple game. Have everyone take turns describing one thing that made them mad; one that made them sad; and one that made them glad during the day.

NO MATERIALS NEEDED

Money Bags

FamilyFun *contributor Susan Fox beats the "Are we there yets" this way.* She suggests giving each of your kids a bag containing ten pennies, nickels, or dimes (you might have to use dollar bills with teens and preteens). Every time a child asks any variation of the question "When will we be there?" she must pay a parent a coin from her bag. Kids get to keep whatever coins are left at the trip's end. You also can let them earn back coins they've relinquished by performing various noble tasks, such as escorting a younger sibling to the bathroom.

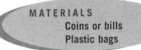

MATERIALS
Coins or bills
Plastic bags

ROAD FOOD
A Good Egg

Hard-boiled eggs are a perfect road food if you peel them first, wrap them in plastic, and chill them. Here's a foolproof recipe: Place eggs in a saucepan and cover with water. Bring to a boil, reduce heat, and simmer 15 minutes (add 2 minutes if eggs are straight from the fridge). Plunge eggs into cold water. Keep in the cooler or eat within two hours.

FAMILY TESTERS
OUR HISTORY

Empty your photograph and pamphlet junk drawer and give it to your kids along with a glue stick, markers, and an empty notebook. Invite them to create their own version of your family history. You'll get some hilarious juxtapositions.
Ariel Duckler-Levy, Great Neck, New York

Town and City Scavenger Hunts

AROUND TOWN

If you're driving through one of America's many wonderful small towns, encourage your kids to search out the details. Be on the lookout for these:

- A building more than 100 years old
- A humorous or out-of-date billboard
- A place where an important event occurred
- A dirt road
- A statue or outdoor sculpture
- A street with a great view
- A house painted in three colors
- A graveyard
- A lake or pond
- A factory where an everyday item is made
- A street named after someone famous
- A shop you've never visited
- A Yield sign
- A footbridge
- A tree with seed or fruit on its branches
- A shop that sells ice-cream cones

IN THE CITY

Stuck in downtown traffic? Pull out this list to help pass the time.

- A person with blue or purple hair
- A CD store
- A building with more than twenty stories
- A person with a hat bigger than his head
- A dog with a coat
- A dog with a bow
- A roller skater
- A bicycle messenger

CLASSICS
PADIDDLE

This little crowd-pleaser keeps kids of all ages going for journeys of an hour or a week. Start with the simple Padiddle concept, in which you all try to be the first to shout "Padiddle" whenever a car with only one working headlight comes into view.

Then expand on the concept, coming up with other words for things you see along the way. You might start to call out "Moopuddle" as soon as you spot a cow. Or you may decide to say "Ugherjunker" every time you see an abandoned car.

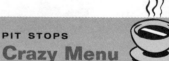

PIT STOPS
Crazy Menu

On a paper restaurant menu, take turns crossing out key words. Then have your kids read aloud the new and often grotesque combinations they've created. Anyone for Pepperoni Cake with Strawberry Lettuce?

- A police car
- A taxicab
- A brass plaque
- A store with a foreign name
- A scary movie marquee
- A church

URBAN ARCHITECTURE HUNT

Part of the fun in this hunt is in learning about the things you are looking for. The search items are more sophisticated, so try this in parent-kid or older-younger child teams.

- Porch
- Gargoyle
- Column
- Arch
- Symmetrical building
- Asymmetrical building
- Garden sculpture
- Fountain
- House with two front doors
- Eyebrow window
- Dormer
- Stained-glass window
- Bay window

- Chimney
- Brick building
- Building made of wood
- Building made of metal and glass
- Building you think is beautiful
- Building you would never want to live in

MATERIALS
Paper and pencils

ROAD FOOD

BREAKFAST ON THE FLY

For a hassle-free early start on a long day's drive, shuffle your kids into the car in their pajamas and have a nutritious backseat break- fast ready for them when they wake up. Here's a menu.

Quick Breakfast Shake
2   frozen bananas
1/2   cup berries or other fruit
1/2   cup milk or orange juice
1/2   cup yogurt (optional)

Puree all the ingredients together in a food processor or blender and pour into individual ther- moses. Makes 2 servings.

Bagels with Strawberry Butter
1/2   cup butter, softened
1/4   cup strawberry jam

To make the bagel spread, blend the butter and jam together by hand or in a food processor. (You also can make flavored cream cheese by adding 1/4 cup of your favorite jam to 1/2 cup of softened cream cheese.)

The Signs

Teach your kids a few phrases in American Sign Language:

I'm Hungry — First, sign "I" by making a fist with the pinky sticking up and pulling it toward your chest with the pinky facing out. Sign "hungry" with your hand positioned as if wrapped around a cup held to the middle of your chest a few inches below the neck, fingers pointing toward you. The hand moves downward to stomach level once.

Be Quiet! — This phrase is a single sign. Hold your hand with the four fingers against each other and the thumb below them, forming a beak (like making a shadow duck). Place the hand in front of the mouth and pull back, with the thumb and fingers pulling apart and coming together as the hand moves away from the face.

COUNTING GAME
Meet Your Make

Time for a new car? Let this game of chance determine whether it will be a Porsche or a Pinto. Let each player pick a number between ten and fifty. Now, count every car coming toward you in the opposite lane until you get to your numbers. Expect cheers from the little brother who picked twenty-seven and sees his car, a bright yellow Humvee, and groans from big sister who picked number thirty-two and discovers that on her 16th birthday she'll be driving a 1976 Gremlin.

NO MATERIALS NEEDED

Newspaper Scavenger Hunt

Dreaming of a little undisturbed newspaper reading while your spouse has the wheel? Try this activity. Toss unwanted or finished sections into the backseat along with a list of ten items your kids can search for, and tear out of, the paper. Depending on your kids' ages, you can have them look for words, such as *discount, hurry, theater, robbery,* and *hot,* or pictures, such as a truck, a television, or a food product with fruit in it. Young children can tear out rainbow colors from the funnies section. (If you'll be going grocery shopping, you might just include ten items from your list and let your kids do a little bargain hunting.)

MATERIALS
Paper and pencils
Daily newspaper

ROAD FOOD
Faux Cookies

Preheat the oven to 350°. Place bread slices on a cookie sheet and top with thin slices of cheese. Cut out shapes using cookie cutters. Heat until cheese starts to bubble. Cool.

Colorful Commentary

"Look, Mom, it's Superman. And he's just jumped in front of a train." *If it sometimes seems your kids are constantly seeing things out the car window that you just missed, this game is your chance for payback.* To play, everyone except the driver must close their eyes. Now the driver begins to narrate a play-by-play of everything going on outside the car. If a player suspects the driver is lying about what he sees, that player should immediately declare a challenge, open her eyes, and observe the truth. Everyone else's eyes remain closed. If the accusing player has caught the driver in a lie, she becomes the commentator for the next round. If the driver really did see a dog in a bicycle basket, the accuser is out for the duration of that round.

NO MATERIALS NEEDED

CLASSICS
FICTIONARY

This classic parlor game is just right for a road trip. One player picks an obscure word in the dictionary and writes down the definition on a slip of paper. Each of the other players makes up a definition and writes it on a slip of paper. The first player collects the definitions and reads them aloud (including the real one), then asks for votes on which is correct. Players who win votes for their fake definitions score a point each; if a player guesses the correct definition, he receives a point. The player with the most points wins.

Where Do You Hear It?

This game can deteriorate quickly, warns FamilyFun contributor Susan Fox, but it's guaranteed to hold everyone's attention — particularly toddlers and teens — and inspire some hearty chuckles. One person mimics a sound and everyone tries to guess where this sound or function is performed. For example, if you make the sound of computer keys tapping, the answer would be "in the office," or wherever the computer lives. If you make the sound of a tea kettle whistling, the answer would be "in the kitchen." (Unfortunately, a lot of the answers tend to be "in the bathroom.")

NO MATERIALS NEEDED

FAMILY TESTERS

POST OFFICE

Instead of tossing your daily ration of junk mail, squirrel it away unopened for your next trip. Throw it in the backseat and let your kids play post office. Jennifer, 9, likes to sort by state. Shelby, 5, likes the stickers in sweepstakes entries.

Minnie Huster, Lake City, Iowa

Chocolate Clusters

Every rest stop tempts a kid to the candy machines, but with these sweet treats, you can satisfy their cravings without spending 75 cents a pop.

Microwave 1 cup chocolate chips on high for 1 to 2 minutes, or until melted. Stir in 1 cup nuts or chopped, dried fruit, and drop by teaspoonful onto a waxed paper–lined baking sheet. Refrigerate until firm.

CLASSICS
RACE TO 20

Two players take turns counting to twenty. On each turn, a player can say one or two numbers. (If the first says "One," the second might say "Two, three.") Try to force your opponent to reach twenty first.

Jeane Dixon Wanna-Bes

Think about it: Your kids are always asking you to foretell the future, from what will be at your destination to exactly what time you'll be there. Turn the tables on them this vacation. At the beginning of each day's travels, have everyone fill out a list of predictions. What time will we arrive at our destination? What will the weather be like? Will there be a pool? Will the ice machine have ice in cubes or ice in slices? Will we see any deer along the road?

Now seal the predictions in an envelope and put them away until dinnertime, when they'll serve as great conversation starters.

MATERIALS
Paper and pencils
Envelopes

FAMILY TESTERS
ART MEDLEY

To keep our three boys, Justin, Alex, and Robin (who are 10, 8, and 7 years old), occupied while we are driving, my husband and I came up with a musical game. We record a medley of songs — pop, classical, country, even some yodeling — on a cassette. Then I cut from magazines pictures associated with the music, and the boys try to match photos with songs.

Sherry Kerber
Granite City, Illinois

Picture This

Get your little chatterboxes to quiet down with this game suggested by FamilyFun *editor Priscilla Totten who, along with her eleven siblings, helped her parents* come up with creative methods for stopping the noise. When the din builds to a crescendo, tell your kids you will entertain comments, questions, and suggestions only in picture form for a prescribed amount of time.

MATERIALS
Drawing paper
Crayons or pencils

She Shows Seashells

My family loves to spend our vacations at the beach. We always collect many seashells that we think are pretty enough to frame so that we can make them part of our annual summer photo collage. Once we get home, Danielle, 9, and Tiffany and Stephanie, 7-year-old twins, pick out their favorite shells and glue them on the edge of an 8- by 10-inch frame. We cut up vacation photos and assemble the collage, then attach labels to caption the pictures. We hang the pictures proudly every year.

**Lorene Hall
Starke, Florida**

COOL IT!

Whether you use a cooler, an insulated bag or box, or Tupperware, here's how to keep snacks cool without messy, melting ice.

- Add frozen juice boxes.
- Make sandwiches on frozen bread.
- Pack some frozen grapes.
- Include a smoothie frozen in a tightly sealed container.
- Use sealed ice packs.

PIT STOPS
COLORS

At rest areas, I get my girls moving by giving them colored bits of paper and taking them on a color hunt. You can also use the color samples paint stores give out.

**Sheri Kinnett
Bailey, Colorado**

SEARCHING GAME
Counting Cows

NO MATERIALS NEEDED

This easy activity can have a soporific side effect — your kids might start drifting off counting cows instead of sheep. Play as individuals or teams. First rule: You can only count cows on your side of the road. Second rule: Stop counting at a previously agreed upon destination. To play: Count cows on your side, trying to have the highest number when you reach your destination. The caveat: Pass a cemetery on your side and you must start back at zero.

If there aren't any cows along your route, try counting mailboxes, phone booths, or tumbleweeds.

Picasso at the Zoo

Some of your kids' favorite animals could be ones that never existed. First, have your children draw in boxes of equal dimensions nine animals — include a chicken, a monkey, and an elephant, for instance. Then cut their drawings horizontally in thirds and mix and match the different pieces. Now they can make up names, such as "henmophant," for their newly created beasties.

MATERIALS
Crayons or markers
Drawing paper
Safety scissors

COPILOTS
Taskees

When our family goes on vacation, we assign each of our seven children an important task for the duration of the trip, one that will make each child an active part of planning. On a trip to Orlando, Florida, these were their assignments.

Sylvia, age 15, navigator and accountant, kept track of mileage, maps, and money; TamiSue, 13, photographer, had to use two rolls of film a day; Joshua, 10, auto mechanic, pumped gas and checked oil and tire pressure; Bryan, 7, mailman, got postcards and stamps and mailed the cards kids write to themselves each day (see page 8); Libby, 7, dietitian, made sure the cooler was stocked; Andrew, 6, activities coordinator and music director, was solely in charge of the tape player; and Katie, 5, referee, settled all road disputes.

Wendy Lira, Alma, Kansas

The Not-So-Newlywed Game

If your kids enjoy playing Mom off against Dad — or vice versa — they'll love this game. While Dad is driving, have your kids write up a premarital questionnaire for Mom. What was Dad wearing the first time you saw each other? What exactly did you say? What did you think of his haircut? What did your parents think about him? Mom must answer the questions quietly in writing. When Mom and Dad switch driving duties, have Dad answer the same questions. Now the fun begins. Kids get to compare answers out loud, and may even ask Mom and Dad to guess how the other responded before the answer is revealed. Be warned: Your kids will probably try to sneak some none-of-their-business questions into the test (Who were you dating when you met Dad?). In this case, parental privilege kicks in — refuse to answer on the grounds of self-incrimination.

> **MATERIALS**
> **Paper and pencils**

CLASSICS
And Don't Forget . . . ⭐

Word Stretch: Give your child a word challenge by asking her to make as many words as she can from the letters in a phrase such as Are we there yet? or When will we be at the zoo?

Pack a Picnic: Hone your children's memory skills by taking turns choosing items to bring on a picnic. "I'm going on a picnic, and I'm packing berries," the first player might say. "I'm going on a picnic, and I'm packing berries and chocolate whoopie pies," the second player might add. And so on until a player forgets the order (it's a good idea to have a parent keeping track on paper).

Black Jaguars

This is a game to launch whenever you pull out of a rest area. Have each player write down the make and color of one car *other than* red, white, and blue — a green Mercedes, say, or a black Jaguar. The first player to spy his or her car gets to choose where to sit after the next rest stop. Each type spotted is deleted from further competition. Start over after every stop.

MATERIALS
Paper and pencils

FAMILY TESTERS

I M ABLE

When my preschool-age son was learning his letters and numbers, we practiced by taking turns calling out those from the license plates on the cars in front of us.

Tammie T. Bullard
Memphis, Tennessee

WANDA THE WIZARD #2

The wizard supplies pencil and paper and asks her subject to do the following:

1. List numbers 1 through 10 across the top of the page.
2. Choose any two numbers under 100 and put the first under the number 1 and the second under the number 2.
3. Add them together and place the sum under number 3.
4. Add the numbers under 2 and 3 to get number 4, under 3 and 4 to get number 5, and so on until the tenth column has been filled.
5. Add all the answers and secretly write the total on another piece of paper.

The wizard reveals the same answer by taking a shortcut: she simply multiplies the total in column 7 by 11.

Animate It

Cartoonists love the chance to see their work in motion. And it's easy to accomplish. You can create an animated flip book with a pad of Post-it notes. Just draw a simple, changing illustration on each page — a ball rolling across the pages, a flower growing up and blooming, or a frog leaping.

To try two-frame animation, first draw a sad face looking straight ahead on a 2½-inch square of paper. Then draw the same face, wide-eyed, with mouth open and tongue sticking out, on the back side of the paper. Make a small slit in the top of a drinking straw and slide the paper into it. Now roll the straw back and forth in your palms, which will turn the drawing into a tiny drama.

> **MATERIALS**
> Post-it notes pad
> Drawing paper
> Pencils or pens
> Drinking straw

COPILOTS
Call Ahead

Besides scouting resources at your library, call or write to city chambers of commerce and state tourism boards for information about your destination. Let your kids make lists of the things they hope to see and let each child pick one activity to do each day (parents have veto power over monster truck rallies, of course).

Who Lives There?

Travel exposes your family to new places and different styles of living. As you pass a lime-green house with a yard full of plastic pink flamingos and a working waterwheel, it's hard not to wonder what type of family lives there. Why not run with that? Suggest that your kids speculate on who lives inside the houses you pass and what they might be doing at that moment. Perhaps the people in the green house invented mint chocolate chip ice cream. Perhaps they have seven children and three pets — a Lhasa apso, an iguana, and a Persian cat wearing a pink leather collar. If it's dinnertime, perhaps they're gathered around the kitchen table enjoying tuna casserole topped with potato chips that will be followed by a dessert of cherries flambé. They'll be playing a game of Pictionary after dinner and, well, you get the idea.

NO MATERIALS NEEDED

DID YOU REMEMBER?

Toiletry items:
toothbrush, toothpaste, hairbrush, shampoo, shaving equipment, deodorant

Rain gear:
umbrella, boots, slicker

All-purpose layers:
sweatshirt, sweater, long-sleeve cover-up, long underwear

Emergency equipment:
flashlight, extra batteries, medical kit, medicine, alarm clock, prescription medicine

Sun items:
sunglasses (kids', too), hat, sunscreen

Special fun stuff:
bathing suit, hiking boots, tennis shoes and racket, snorkel gear

Essential papers:
tickets, identification (kids', too), passports and visas, traveler's checks

In the Bag

Whenever her family is going on a long car trip, FamilyFun *reader Pat Peck of Sanford, North Carolina, packs a special bag of what she calls "oddities."* Just empty your junk drawer into a bag, suggests Pat, and when the mood strikes (or the "you're-on-my-side" squabbling starts), reach into the bag, pull out one thing, and pass it around. Request that each passenger transform the item by play-acting with it. An empty paper towel tube turns into a pirate telescope; a paper napkin is folded into a villain's mustache; a ski cap becomes a horse's feed bag; and a colander is now a robot's head.

MATERIALS
A dozen items from your family junk or gadgets drawer

Echo Echo

Little kids adore nonsense words, and this activity is sure to hit their silly bones. To play, a leader sings a nonsensical made-up song line, such as "Shabba, shabba, woopy doo-doo." The rest of the car repeats the line. Then the leader adds on another line, such as "Gabba-gabba hey hey hey!" The other players sing it back, and so on, until an echo song has been created (when it just feels done or everyone dissolves into a puddle of laughter).

For younger kids, just creating and singing goofy tunes over and over will keep them occupied. For older kids, you might want to play this as an add-on copycat game, with different players adding one new line of nonsense each, and everyone challenged to remember and repeat the order.

Warning: Noise- and nonsense-sensitive parents might want to consider introducing this game only when they know they'll be getting out of the car soon!

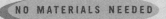

NO MATERIALS NEEDED

FAMILY TESTERS

FANTASY ISLAND

To keep my kids (Howard, 8, Jerry, 7, and Ann, 6) from getting too rowdy when they're in close quarters, I mark off a territory for each. Then I tell them they are each on an island and the islands can't talk to one another. I have them cut out paper fish to write messages on. I put paper clips on the fish, toss them on the seat of the car, and let the kids use magnets on a string to go fishing as a means of quiet communication. I cut out sharks for myself: any message from a shark must be attended to by all anglers.

Sharon Wright
Lansing, Michigan

Fly-Time Scavenger Hunts

You end up with a lot of idle time when you travel by air. Scavenger hunts are an easy way to spend those hours calmly.

IN THE AIRPORT

You don't want anyone lost in the crowd, so set off in parent-child teams to find the following:

- A used boarding pass
- A brochure for a frequent flyer program

- A child holding a doll
- A person carrying four pieces of luggage
- An abandoned sports section of *USA Today*
- A piece of penny candy
- 3 red-haired people
- 4 pilots
- 2 courtesy carts

ON THE AIRPLANE

Find these items individually or together:

- Cars

- Railroad tracks
- Swimming pool
- A cloud
- Another airplane
- A mountain range below
- A lake
- An ocean
- Someone speaking in a foreign language
- A person with hair that's two different colors
- A person in a uniform
- A father holding a baby
- A person in an apron

- Somebody sleeping
- Someone sewing or knitting
- A person wearing socks without shoes
- A vegetarian meal
- A laptop computer
- A mustache
- Wire-rimmed glasses
- A red dress
- A briefcase
- A soda pop can
- A Walkman radio
- A pillow and blanket

AIRBORNE
Surprise Presents

To break up the boredom, and to keep a wiggly child happily seated, fill a bag with wrapped surprises to give as "presents" during your flight. Your bag could contain some of these items:

- Treats such as fruit that comes in its own packaging — bananas, oranges, and so on; their favorite pretzels, cookies, and crackers (or the Zesty Orange Twists on page 73); jelly candies, which won't melt; and fruit roll-ups (recipe at right).

- Toys that are old favorites and

- Candy
- A detective novel
- A cellular phone
- A blue tie

MATERIALS
Paper and pencils

ROAD FOOD
Fruit Leather

These tangy roll-ups are one kind of fruit that keeps well and doesn't bruise.

1	24-ounce jar of applesauce
10	dried apricots
1/2	teaspoon cinnamon

Preheat the oven to 150°. Combine all ingredients in a blender and puree until very smooth. Oil a 9- by 13-inch cookie sheet. Pour the puree onto the pan and shake gently from side to side until it is evenly distributed. Bake for 5 to 6 hours. The leather is done when it is bendable, no longer sticky, and slightly transparent. Once cool, cut it into strips while it is still in the pan. Lay each strip on a piece of plastic wrap. Roll it up with the plastic and store in a covered container.

those that are new and especially distracting (you can buy brand-new coloring books, puzzles, and magnetic games or borrow some from friends).

- Books — those your child has read a thousand times and those you have recently borrowed from the library.
- Story tapes and a personal cassette player for each child, so he or she can hear all the songs from *Aladdin* fifty times, but fellow passengers (and you) won't have to.

Token of Appreciation

*Of course, it would be terrific if your kids
would just spontaneously start to name all
the things they are grateful for, but it's
not likely to happen. You can elicit such conversation, however, with this variation on
an activity from* FamilyFun *reader Margo
Miller of Duluth, Georgia, and her three
boys.* Find a simple totem, such as a rock,
pinecone, or even a stuffed animal, and
tell your family that it is a special thanks-
giving and wish-receiving token. Starting
with yourself, hold the item in your hand
and tell your kids one thing for which
you are most grateful. Pass it around the
family, letting every member have an
opportunity to give thanks for something.

Once the token has been held by everyone once, pass it around the circle again.
This time, family members get to make a
wish for something they'd like to come
true that year. This is an especially mean-
ingful game to play during holiday travel
and may well become a family tradition.

MATERIALS
A rock, pinecone,
or other icon

Who's Next?

What do Charlie Brown and Brad Pitt have in common? The first letter of Charlie's last name is the first letter of Brad's first name. In this word game that can eat away miles, a player starts by naming a celebrity or a person known to everyone in the car — say, Michael Jackson. The next person has to name a person whose first name begins with *J*, such as Jane Seymour. Now the search is on for a celebrity name beginning with an *S*. If you offer an answer that has a first and last name beginning with the same letter — such as Charlie Chaplin — the next person will have to come up with another double *C* name, and so on until you are stumped. Once you're stuck, you're out. Whoever's out last starts a new game.

NO MATERIALS NEEDED

FAMILY TESTERS
Family Flash Cards

We make a set of flash cards with photos of family members on the front and info about how they're related to us and one another on the back. It's the perfect thing to play with on the way to a family reunion. **Mary Jones, Wichita, Kansas**

ROAD FOOD
THE MASTER GORP LIST

It doesn't have to be just Good Old Raisins and Peanuts. Try any or all of these items.

Peanuts	Dried cherries	Rice cereal	Butterscotch chips
Raisins	Dried cranberries	Sunflower seeds	Coconut
Dried apricots	Banana chips	Pretzels	Dates
Dried prunes	Oat cereal	Chocolate chips	Cashews

18 Wheels and Counting

Counting games are perfect for families with kids spanning a wide range of ages. Even preschoolers can usually count, and if your family is counting something that can be challenging to find, you all can have fun. In this tallying game, you make a list of numbers from two to eighteen and try to find vehicles with two, three, four, and on up to eighteen tires — crossing each number off as you find it. The game is easier than it sounds: don't forget trailers, spares, baby carriages, and cars with bike racks. If you spot a trailer hauling new cars from the factory, it counts as a wild card, and you can cross off any number you want. This is best played in teams or just counting as a family, and it works best when you are on a long journey.

MATERIALS
Paper and pencils

FAMILY TESTERS

TREAD ON ME

Before a long car trip, we use chalk to write the names of our four children on the side of a tire: one on top, one on bottom, and one on either side. When we stop, the child whose name sits on the pavement gets a special privilege, such as his choice of seat, music, or dinner destination. The kids have fun trying to guess whose name will come up (or down) next.

Cherlyn Call, Sunrise, Florida

The Clapper

Sometimes car travel makes even the sanest parents and kids feel just plain desperate. That's when you need an energetic game like The Clapper. Make sure, though, that you have earplugs with you and that your destination is in sight. You won't want this one to go on too long. To play, take turns clapping out the pacing and syllables of the words in well-known songs. The first person to name that beat becomes the car's next clapper. Starting clappers should bear in mind that this game works best if you choose a tune that has repeating lyrics (so listeners get a second chance) and enough changes in pacing and multisyllabic words to clue in listeners to the song. "Happy Birthday," "Bingo," and "Old MacDonald" are great starting tunes; "Don't Cry for Me Argentina" is not.

NO MATERIALS NEEDED

ROAD FOOD

GRANOLA BARS

These energy-boosters make a good mid-morning pick-me-up.

$3/4$	cup creamy peanut butter
$1/2$	cup plus 2 tablespoons honey
2	cups granola
1	cup old-fashioned oatmeal
1	cup raisins or chopped dried apricots
$1/2$	cup sunflower seeds
$1/2$	cup chopped walnuts or peanuts
2	eggs, slightly beaten
2	cups crispy rice cereal

Preheat oven to 325°. Grease a 13- by 9- by 2-inch baking pan. In a saucepan over low heat, melt the peanut butter and honey. Cool. In a large bowl, mix the granola, oatmeal, raisins or apricots, sunflower seeds, and walnuts or peanuts. Stir in the peanut butter and honey mixture to coat. Slowly mix in the eggs. Gently stir in the rice cereal and press the mixture into the prepared pan. Bake for 20 to 30 minutes, or until lightly browned on the edges. Cool, cut into squares, and wrap individually. Keep cool.

What Do People Do All Day

WEATHER WISE

Put your kids in charge of tracking the weather during your vacation. Let them tune in to weather reports as you travel along in the car and listen for weather updates from the pilots when you're in a plane. Also, go to your local library before your trip and check out guides on various types of clouds. That should keep them occupied as they stare out the windows trying to identify clouds and what they mean for the weather.

If one of those clouds opens up, encourage your kids to have raindrop races. Just identify which drop at the top of the car window is yours. Then race it against the others to the bottom of the window.

Engage your kids in a little early career counseling. Write down a bunch of different occupations — doctor, lawyer, actor, and so forth — on separate slips of paper and let your kids take turns drawing one slip each and then silently acting out what they think this person does all day. (You may be alarmed by your kids' views of the working world after playing this game, particularly if they decide to portray your job as simply kicking back, talking on the phone, and arranging for lunch.) The first person to guess the occupation draws the next slip.

MATERIALS
Paper and pencils

CLASSICS

Gum Chains

You may not break the world's record for longest gum wrapper chain (18,721 feet), but you can pass time trying. (Of course, you'll have to save up gum wrappers — from the standard stick variety — before your vacation.) To start, tear the first wrapper in half the long way. Fold in the long sides of one strip so they line up in the center, then fold it in half on the line. Fold the short ends so they meet in the center and fold in half again. Repeat the folding for the next wrapper. Now slide the link into the folds of the other strip, and keep repeating.

Finger Puppets

Desperate times can call for measures like this one, when you break the Don't write on yourself! *rule.* Pass your kids any unwanted makeup in your bag and invite them to paint their fingertips. They can color faces, hair, hats, scarves, and clothing on their fingers, then put on a puppet show. End your activity by heading for a rest area and a soap-and-water scrubbing session.

MATERIALS
Mom's makeup bag

PACKING
ON A ROLL

Get your kids excited about packing for themselves by giving them each their own suitcase and backpack to be responsible for. Stencil or sew each child's name on his luggage, then let him decorate the bags however he likes, using stickers, markers, or patches.

Let them pack for themselves (see page 23), concentrating on what to bring rather than on what won't wrinkle. One surprisingly effective and fun technique is to let them just roll everything up!

COPILOTS
Q & A

Laminate a map of your route, then create question-and-answer cards keyed to highlights along the way. Play with them like flash cards.

Emergency Measures!

Need enough peace and quiet to figure out where you took that wrong turn? Resort to these tried-and-true emergency measures:

- Tell your kids to use a blanket to create a back-seat car fort.
- Time who can be quiet the longest.

- Ask your kids to communicate only by using their fingers to write words on each other's backs.
- See who (besides the driver) can hold his or her breath the longest.

MATERIALS
A blanket

FAMILY TESTERS
FREE PHOTOS

We gather pamphlets and brochures from all the places we visit. Once home, you can cut out the pictures and add them to vacation scrapbooks.

Heidi Gaquin
Woonsocket, Rhode Island

Tongue-Twister Tournament

Who can forget Sally's seashells or that wood-chucking woodchuck? Both of these classics are a testament to the enduring popularity of the tongue twister. For your family tongue-twister tournament, begin by making up ten (or more) tongue tanglers.

Just choose a letter, then write down a dozen words that begin with that letter in columns of nouns, proper nouns, adjectives, and verbs. Next, mix them up until they make some semblance of sense. Choosing the letter *W,* for instance, could result in the twister "Which witch with warts would Wanda wake?" or "Willy wondered which white wine Wally would want?"

Once you have ten true tanglers, let the games begin. Who can say the twisters the fastest without error? Who can say them the most times in a row? Who can make up the longest tongue twister? A story that features all tongue twisters?

If you have trouble coming up with ten twisters on your own, fill the holes with some of these classics:

- Rubber baby buggy bumper.
- Sally sells seashells down by the seashore.
- How much wood would a woodchuck chuck if a woodchuck could chuck wood?
- Twelve twins twirled twelve twigs twelve times.
- Eight gray geese grazed gaily in Greece.
- *FamilyFun's Games on the Go* gets good families farther faster.

MATERIALS
Paper and pencils

CLASSICS
Toys to Go

FamilyFun contributor Carolyn Shapiro lists five top travel toys:

Travel Etch A Sketch by Ohio Art (800-641-6226) is a smaller version of the erasable magnetic drawing board.

SS Noah by Pockets of Learning (800-635-2994) is a pillow, toy, and stuffed animal in one.

6-in-1 Travel Magnetic Games by Pressman (800-800-0298) gives you chess, checkers, backgammon, Chinese checkers, Parcheesi, and snakes and ladders.

Back-spin by Binary Arts (703-971-3401) challenges kids to match thirty-five balls with their designated colors. It's the kind of hypnotic puzzle only a child can master.

Secret Highway Messages

The young conspiracy theorists in your family (almost all 8-year-olds) will love the idea that you are being sent secret messages by the highway department. To decode the missives, you must write down the first letter of every official road sign you see until you have five to seven letters. Then break the code as follows.

The first letters stand for words. A series of signs beginning with the letters *B, T, R, O, D* could send the troubling message Barbara Turn Right On the Double. Or, it might mean something more innocuous and cryptic, like Better Take Red One, Dad. It's up to your family to decide, but don't be surprised if the highway department ends up sending you a message similar to the one your kids have been nagging you about recently.

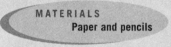

MATERIALS
Paper and pencils

KEEPSAKES

A LARGER-THAN-LIFE JOURNAL

Last summer, we decided to record my 12-year-old daughter's vacation adventures on a mural instead of in a scrapbook. From a large roll of butcher paper, we cut a long strip and tacked it along one inside wall of our garage. In a nearby basket, we put crayons, markers, scissors, and tape. As the weeks passed, Cindy attached pictures, post-cards, and ticket stubs from the events she had attended. She also had family and friends add to her mural when they came for a visit. At the end of the season, she had a jam-packed collage of her favorite summer moments.

Sheryl Zarnowiec
Edmond, Oklahoma

Exit Now

You're in a new city, on a highway, nearing your destination, and you don't want to miss your exit. But the rapid-fire flow of Knock Knock jokes in the backseat is becoming seriously distracting. As you see Exit signs, instruct everyone to close their eyes and try to sense when you'll be at the first exit listed. Each person shouts "Now" when she thinks you're close. The person with the best guess wins; keep playing until you are safely off the highway and headed for dinner, inspired conversation, and a comfy bed.

NO MATERIALS NEEDED

Lunch Spreads

An assortment of spreads in plastic containers makes an instant lunchtime buffet with bagels, baguettes, rice cakes, or crackers. Try hummus, nut butters (peanut, cashew, or almond), jelly, flavored cream cheeses, or black bean dip.

ARTISTIC

Whenever we stop at museums, we have a method for getting our kids to pay attention to the exhibits. We proceed immediately to the gift shop, buy postcards, and tell our kids the rules of the game. For every postcard they match with an exhibit inside, they earn one dollar.

**Christy Macy
Baltimore, Maryland**

Paper Cup Puppets

While you wait for the bill or while your child is still playing with the last of his spaghetti at a rest area eatery, turn your empty paper drink cups into puppets. Using a serrated dinner knife or a pair of manicure scissors (parents only), make ears and a nose by drawing three squares onto the cup, then cutting each square on three sides. Pull out the tabs you've created and finish off the puppets with paper napkin clothes your kids can color in the car.

Category Index

Category Index

Category Index

Alphabetical Index

Also from *FamilyFun* and 🌹HYPERION

FamilyFun's Cookbook, by Deanna F. Cook and the experts at *FamilyFun*, is a collection of more than 500 irresistible recipes for you and your kids, from healthy snacks to birthday cakes to dinners everyone in the family can enjoy.

FamilyFun's Crafts, by Deanna F. Cook and the experts at *FamilyFun*, is a step-by-step guide to more than 500 of the best crafts and activities to do with your kids.

FamilyFun's Cookies for Christmas, by Deanna F. Cook and the experts at *FamilyFun*, is a collection of more than 50 holiday recipes for you and your kids.

FamilyFun's Parties, by Deanna F. Cook and the experts at *FamilyFun*, is a complete party planner with more than 500 games, activities, and foods for birthdays, holidays, and every day.